Henry Blackburn

Art in the mountains: the story of the passion play

Henry Blackburn

Art in the mountains: the story of the passion play

ISBN/EAN: 9783742884329

Manufactured in Europe, USA, Canada, Australia, Japa

Cover: Foto ©Thomas Meinert / pixelio.de

Manufactured and distributed by brebook publishing software (www.brebook.com)

Henry Blackburn

Art in the mountains: the story of the passion play

The Oberammergau Passion Play.

ART IN THE MOUNTAINS

The Story of the Passion Play.

BY

HENRY BLACKBURN,

EDITOR OF 'ACADEMY NOTES;' AUTHOR OF 'ARTISTS AND ARABS,'
'BRETON FOLK,' 'THE PYRENEES,' ETC.

WITH NUMEROUS ILLUSTRATIONS,

AND AN APPENDIX OF

INFORMATION FOR TRAVELLERS.

LONDON:
SAMPSON LOW, MARSTON, SEARLE, & RIVINGTON,
CROWN BUILDINGS, 188 FLEET STREET.
1880.

PREFACE.

THE production of the Passion Play at Oberammergau in 1880 (which is only performed once in ten years), and the extraordinary interest attaching to the last performances, have decided the publishers to reissue the following record of the *Passionspiel*.

In turning over the leaves of 'Art in the Mountains'—written when this wonderful drama was fresh in men's minds, and when its beauty and importance as a work of religious art was only half understood—the author finds little to alter, or amend. The record as it stands is true to the letter, and the programme is the same for 1880 as in former years.

It is interesting to learn from private letters, that the worthy inhabitants of Oberammergau are preparing for their work in the same earnest, devotional spirit as in 1870, and that they were in no sense demoralised by the popularity of the last performances. There will be a few changes in the distribution of the parts, but Joseph Mair and Gregor Lechner (whose portraits are engraved on pp. 77 and 103) will again take the principal parts.

The Passion Play will be performed, generally on Sundays, from May 17th to September 26th. (*See* dates on p. 169.)

March 1880.

CONTENTS.

	PAGE
CHAP. I.—IN MUNICH	11
CHAP. II.—ON THE ROAD	27
CHAP. III.—AT OBERAMMERGAU	50
CHAP. IV.—THE PASSION PLAY—PART I.	66
CHAP. V.—THE PASSION PLAY—PART II.	109
CHAP. VI.—THE ACTORS AND THE AUDIENCE	137
CHAP. VII.—CONCLUDING NOTES	157

APPENDIX.

PROGRAMME OF THE PASSION PLAY	165
LIST OF PERFORMERS IN 1870 AND IN 1880	167
MAP OF ROUTE	168
INFORMATION FOR TRAVELLERS	169

LIST OF ILLUSTRATIONS.

		PAGE
JOSEPHA FLUNGER (*Chorus in* 1870)	*frontispiece*	
ON THE MOUNTAINS		21
PEASANTS ON THE ROAD		29
OUR DRIVER		31
A PORTRAIT		32
MOUNTAIN CHALET		35
VIEW OF THE VALLEY OF OBERAMMERGAU		37
A SKETCH IN THE VILLAGE		39
ONE OF THE CROWD		44
THE THEATRE		46
SKETCH OF COSTUME		53
THE NIGHT BEFORE THE PLAY		56
EARLY MASS		58
A SKETCH IN THE VILLAGE		61
LEADER OF THE CHORUS		69
THE CHRISTUS		77
SAINT PETER		81
PHARISEE		85
CAIAPHAS		89
THE MARIA		93
SAINT JOHN		97
JUDAS		103
RABBI		113
PILATE		117
THE CHRISTUS		121
BARABBAS		127
A SKETCH IN THE THEATRE		139
ITALIAN PRIEST		144

ART IN THE MOUNTAINS.

CHAPTER I.

IN MUNICH.

IT was about the end of the month of May 1870 that some curious rumours were abroad in Munich—rumours that created no small commotion in our artistic community. In the cool shade of an atelier in the Gabelsberger Strasse we heard the story that we, who were in "the centre of art" in Europe, and lived in its atmosphere, so to speak, were soon to be beaten on our own ground, and to be excelled by a few poor peasants in the mountains.

We little thought, and certainly did not half believe, that the Bavarian mountains we had watched so often on summer evenings from the old bridge over the Isar—that sent us rain on our thirsty plain, and clouds to shelter us from a sunshine sometimes as fierce as in Italy —could add in any human way to the teaching of our schools. The idea, we all agreed, was monstrous; and it was scouted accordingly. In painting, had we not Piloty and Kaulbach, not to mention a host of others; in music, had we not Wagner; in singing and acting, Stehle, of the "National Theatre"? Could it be possible that Munich which possessed a splendid national collection of pictures and sculpture, an opera and theatre renowned throughout Europe with artists and actors trained in the schools of Greece and Italy—was to be excelled by the peasants of Oberammergau?

But we could not be unaware that during the winter evenings of the last three years these peasants had been eagerly and earnestly at work in preparing a reproduction of the great Passion Play, which, every ten years, they are permitted to perform. Of the elaborate nature and importance of this play we had heard and read in previous years, but none of us, now that it was going to occur again so near our own doors, realised the fact of its artistic merit, and few, we foresee, of those who read these lines will easily believe it.

The question of the morality—and of the good or evil influence of the *Passionsspiel* upon the people, who crowd in thousands from all parts of Germany to see it—will perhaps be answered in the course of the narrative; we will now proceed to tell it from an unbiassed and unprejudiced point of view, adding the opinion of one or two other eye-witnesses, by the aid of which (with the illustrations) the reader may form as complete an idea as possible, without being present at the play.

The history of the Passion Play is soon told. In the year 1633 the village of Oberammergau[1] was desolated with pestilence, caused by the wars of Gustavus Adolphus, and the inhabitants in their distress resolved to represent "once in ten years for ever" the Death and Passion of Christ. They made a solemn vow to do this, and, according to the old chroniclers, "the plague was stayed." In the last century such representations were common throughout Bavaria, but in 1779 they were interdicted by the clergy; ex-

---

[1] Oberammergau is a small village in the Bavarian Tyrol, about sixty miles south-west of Munich. Information about the journey, &c. for the use of visitors to Oberammergau will be found in the Appendix.

cepting only the one at Oberammergau, which, being under the superintendence of the monks of the neighbouring monastery at Ettal and having a special object, was still permitted to be held.

It was during Lent of the year 1870 that Herr Schmid first startled us, in the pages of the *Gartenlaube*,[1] with an account of a visit he had paid to Oberammergau; it was this narrative, and the reports that came from time to time into Munich, of the doings at this mountain village, that decided us to start in a few days for the mountains, so as to be present at the performance on Whitsunday.

Herr Schmid's account of one of the rehearsals is so graphic that we shall do well to preface our own experiences with a short extract. Starting whilst the snow was on the ground—on

---

[1] See *Pall Mall Gazette*, June 10, 1870.

rough roads, past the frozen lake of Starnberg, and through gloomy forests of firs—he arrives one evening, in almost total darkness, at the Schabenwirth, the principal hostelry of the village. Here he was greeted by the sound of a first-rate instrumental band, numbering thirty performers. It was the orchestra, practising the intended prelude of welcome to the audience. The company which formed the audience consisted principally of young men, some of whom were playing quietly at cards, and had otherwise the air of wandering artists. These listeners were mostly intending performers in the play, and, like three-fourths of the Ammergauers, were wood-carvers by trade; whence perhaps a certain air of picturesqueness which they had imparted to the trimming of their hair and beards.

The following morning was a Sunday, and having ascertained that during Lent there was a Sunday acting-rehearsal every week, besides a

Thursday musical rehearsal, Herr Schmid hastens to the abode of the parish priest to try whether it were possible to get a view of the proceedings.

After some difficulty, he obtains the necessary permission, and in the evening is conducted to a long, low apartment, formed by throwing several rooms into one. At a table sits the pastor, Herr Müller, together with his predecessor in the cure, Herr Daisenberger, the author of the present text and arrangement of the Passion Play, who, after a quarter of a century's active work in the Ammergau, has retired upon a small stipend to remain, *emeritus*, in the home to which his heart is given. A villager, with the book open before him, sits ready to act as prompter if needful. The visitor retires softly to a window, and at once feels the magic spell upon him. He shall now tell his own impressions.

"I had already witnessed and borne a part in many stage rehearsals; but at the first glance I saw plainly that this was something very different from a play in the ordinary sense. It was evident, too, whence proceeded the very remarkable effect which the dramatic performance of these simple villagers unquestionably produces on the beholder. In the first place, I felt convinced that the solemnity of the subject, the thrilling import of its mighty tragedy, was present with and above all technical preparations, and took from them the haste, restlessness, and distraction inseparable from dramatic preliminaries in general. These performers are not occupied with the thought that they are acting a play, setting forth, as it were, a representation of certain transactions apart from their own lives. Rather they are putting their whole selves into their assumed parts—they give the utterance of their own simple feeling without semblance of art or study. And in this absence of premeditated effect, this spontaneousness, lies the secret of their truth to nature, and of the impression produced on the beholder. No manager here conducted the arrangement of the scenes, no inspector watched over their succession; nor was any such functionary needed, for all the actors listened and looked their parts when mute, or spoke and moved when the right moment came. Scarcely twice had the prompter to interpose with some trifling correction. Every speech was delivered with precision, every gesture was in order, and, notwithstanding the unfavourable conditions of the temporary stage, even the crowded scenes were performed with a method and accuracy perfectly astonishing."

In the evening Herr Schmid found himself in a small social circle of the villagers. They had got over their shyness of the stranger, and were ready to make him one of themselves with cordial hospitality. There sat the future Peter of the drama, a perfect model for a sculptor, with his bald head, full beard, and venerable aspect; Judas, with pale, shrewd face and intense eyes; Annas, with iron-grey beard and thoughtful melancholy expression. He described them all as simple, open-hearted, sensible men, content with their moderately gainful trade, whose placid lives are marked to them by successive epochs of the Passion Play.

This, and much more (which it would be anticipating to speak of in this chapter), found its way into the German newspapers, giving what appeared to us exaggerated descriptions, and suggesting a thing impossible, that these peasants —whom we had seen so often in their daily occupations of tending flocks and carrying wood for winter fires—could excel in the dramatic art.

We had remembrances, too, of Anna Mary

Howitt's description of the *Passionsspiel* as performed in 1850, in which she mentions that one

ON THE MOUNTAINS.

of the peasants " had studied her part under a well-known Munich actress, and had unfortunately brought away with her theatrical affectation and a miserable air of conceit."

But, as summer approached, the shops in Munich began to be filled with photographs of the principal performers (and with books of the drama with designs by Albert Dürer), which gave an idea of what was going forward; and then friends who had been present on the first day came back with glowing descriptions of the play. We cross-questioned them well as to its merits, and their answers, though varied enough, were in accord as to its excellence and solemnity. The painter had never seen such living pictures, nor the actor such natural acting; the cynic admitted the solemnity of the performance, and the religious impression on the majority was evidently of the most solemn kind.

But those of our party who had been in Spain could not but remember the effect on the mind of witnessing religious plays at Seville and Cordova during the Holy Week; and they could not easily forget the excitement of the audience and the irrelevant and irreverent exclamations of the crowd that rushed to witness the "*Seven Dolors of the Virgin*" and "*El Hombre Dios*" at the theatre at Madrid; a performance sanctioned by priestly patrons, which was principally a vehicle for tinsel and display.

It was too much to expect, perhaps, that any Protestant English people (educated in a severe, undemonstrative, undramatic religious school, where colour, imagination, and passion have little influence) could witness with equanimity the mantilla and the fan flirting in the side boxes, whilst the Saviour of the world was being crowned with thorns before their eyes; and it may even have suited the temper of a Spanish audience best when (as at the theatre in Seville), after the scene representing the last act of Judas in this world, they saw canvas rocks fall asunder and a company of stage devils, vomiting fire, exulting over the fallen traitor.

The accounts which appeared in the newspapers of a Belgian Passion Play which took place in 1870 at Laeken, the summer residence of the King of the Belgians, may be remembered by some readers. An eye-witness of that irreverent performance thus speaks of it:—

"It was under the shadow of the great church at Laeken that our modern miracle-players set up their 'theatre,' their special *raison d'être* being the 'kermesse,' fair, or patron-saint's festival, of the village. The exterior of the theatre, a canvas and lath erection of imposing size, attracted all passers-by, by a flaring advertisement of 'La Passion de N. S. Jésus-Christ,' backed by paintings in a popular style of art, representing scenes from the Gospel History, intermingled with sensational pictures of clowns, harlequins, columbines, and conjurors, accomplishing miracles more marvellous than those of Egypt, including dogs ascending skywards in a shower of fireworks."

Such experiences, and the early history of religious plays both in our own country and in Germany, did not inspire us with enthusiasm or hope as to the result, and were utterly at variance with the accounts from Oberammergau, and the reverential spirit of those engaged in the play.

But there was one description (written years ago) that had made a deeper impression than all the rest. It was of the "chorus of angels" at Oberammergau, of which the writer (Anna Howitt) says:—" A fantastic vision passed across the stage, white tunics glanced in the light, crimson, violet, and azure mantles swept the ground, plumed head-dresses waved in the breeze; it was like a strange flight of fabulous birds;

and as they sang, 'Peace on earth and good-will towards men,' their voices rose towards heaven and echoed amongst the hills."

Could all this, or one-half of this, be true? Was poetry, then, one of the gifts granted to the peasants of Oberammergau? Did imagination, as well as the fine arts, slumber amongst the mountains, to burst forth once in ten years and astonish the world?

A mystery was concealed in the " cloudland " that had hitherto brought us only rain and wood for fires—let us attempt to unravel it.

CHAPTER II.

ON THE ROAD.

E leave Munich by railway at half past six on Friday morning, taking the train by the banks of the Lake of Starnberg to Weilheim. The railway station is crowded with people of all ranks and countries, principally peasants; an idea of the extraordinary costumes of some of the latter may be gathered from the next illustration, drawn by the well-known American artist, Felix Darley.

Soon after leaving Munich, the train begins to wind amongst the hills, darting through green valleys and by the side of a smooth lake; then rushing through a pine wood, and writhing up the mountain-side like some living thing, it darts through a cloud, and comes suddenly upon Weilheim. Here we leave the railway, and, taking one of the common conveyances on the road, the "Stellwagen," or "Bauerwagen," we continue our journey upward, to Oberammergau.

It is 9 o'clock in the morning, and the sun is so powerful that we are glad to spread the covering of our carriage, which is stretched over us like the awnings on boats on the Italian lakes. Our waggon is overladen, of course, and is as slow, uncomfortable, and picturesque, as any vehicle constructed before the days of railways. It is a long and narrow conveyance on four wheels, without springs, roughly formed of long poles and a few cross-pieces of wood, with a double

PEASANTS ON THE WAY.

row of seats down the middle, the driver sitting in front on a sack of provender for the horses; the waggon is drawn by two rough, unkempt, unruly horses taken from the fields, and travels at about four miles an hour.

OUR DRIVER.

But we come to see the people *en voyage*, and must not complain. It is true, we might remonstrate, when the driver gets up a trot over the stones on reaching a village, when our money is shaken out of our pockets, and we tumble against one another in helpless confusion; but it is part of the programme, and we would not miss the jolting for the world. And we should

A PORTRAIT.

not like to have missed sitting opposite to a charming *Fräulein*, with her grace of form half hidden and disguised under a costume so quaint and hideous that nothing but the full-length sketch at page 53 could give the reader any idea of it; and we should not like to have missed—as those must do who travel hence in private carriages—the friendly meeting of this peasant party (twenty-two people, old and young) from all parts of Bavaria, all bent on the same errand; all quietly and deeply interested by anticipation in the great play.

Our journey from Weilheim, a distance of about twenty-seven miles, took eight hours, and cost (we mention this for the benefit of intending travellers) about 5s. each. There were a number of vehicles at the railway station at Weilheim to meet the train; and as we passed through the gates of the old town, we formed a long and picturesque procession winding up the hills.

The road for many miles leads through undulating pasture-land, with corn-fields, and orchards; and here and there, at odd corners, we pass some wayside shrine or hideous statue of the Virgin, before one of which our creaking conveyance stops, and some of the peasants kneel in prayer.

Here, had we time to sketch it, was a picture worth recording. Through the open end of the awning—which arches above our heads, and through which the sunlight streams down on two old women in the waggon, and on the head of our sleepy driver—we can see the figures kneeling at the shrine with its gaudy colouring; behind it a field of Indian corn, and beyond, the mountains, no longer distant, but plainly distinguishable, towering one above the other in dark cloud-like masses. The line of carriages which have gone on before is just disappearing over the brow of a hill, and for the moment we are quiet enough to hear the trickling of a brook and the voices of birds.

We halt at midday at Murnau, a small market-town on the road to Partenkirch and Mittenwald; our way afterwards lying through an open country, studded with scattered hamlets. Towards evening we turn off the high-road, westward, and enter a narrow gorge which might be part of the Tête Noire in Switzerland, and commence an ascent so steep that it is difficult for

even an empty "Stellwagen" to be dragged to the top. There are one or two mountain châlets on the road, and on either side, tall pine trees (some struck by lightning, or by the woodman) lying across the bed of the stream, the Loisach; and through their branches we can see at intervals the peaks of the Zugspitz and the Wetterstein, at a height of 7000 or 8000 feet. On emerging from this romantic gorge, we see amongst the trees a great dark dome, as if the cupola of the Invalides in Paris had been suddenly transported to the mountains of Bavaria. It is the old Benedictine monastery of ETTAL, a relic of the middle ages, now converted into a brewery. Our driver, seeing that we are strangers, recommends us to alight and see some pictures by Tyrolese artists, and "a ceiling by Knoller," and—to taste the beer; but we are all pilgrims bent upon one errand—we will see, or hear of, nothing but the Play.

The road now turns northward, and we approach the little village of Oberammergau which lies scattered in the broad valley of the Amber, about three miles from the monastery. We are almost the last of the procession of carriages, and as

VIEW OF THE VALLEY OF OBERAMMERGAU.

we rumble through the principal street (where there are hardly any people), and our waggon stops with a jolt opposite a house like the one in the illustration, it is difficult, nay almost impossible, to believe that six thousand people can collect here next Sunday.

But we soon see that there is plenty of accommodation for travellers, and that there are (including those in the immediate neighbourhood) at least a hundred houses, some well built of wood and stone. They look clean and bright (many being new this year), and are fitted from top to bottom with beds for travellers. Most of the houses stand in their own piece of garden ground, and the people, who are principally wood-carvers, appear as quiet and simple in their habits as in any other part of the Bavarian Tyrol.

As we enter the village, the peasants are returning from the fields, leading home their cattle, and exchanging rustic greetings and

A STREET IN OBERAMMERGAU.

"Gute Nachts!" as they go to their quiet châlets. There is nothing in appearance to strike a stranger, excepting, perhaps, a certain gravity and dignity of demeanour about the men. The women are attractive and healthy-looking, and the features of some are very striking, but there is nothing so far, either in the people we have seen or in the aspect of Oberammergau, to account for its present importance in the eyes of Germany.

We present a letter of introduction to Madame Georg Lang, the widow of one of the principal people of the place, and soon obtain most comfortable quarters. The house, which has been enlarged and newly fitted up in preparation for an influx of visitors, is also the post-office; on the ground floor there is a sort of bazaar for the sale of wood-carving, also a shop full of groceries and stores. Frau Lang and her daughters manage the whole business. This summer they have turned every available space into bed-rooms, and their dwelling-room is the *salle à manger*. In a warehouse underneath our bed-room are stored away several hundred images of the Christ in various stages of completion—heads and limbs, crowns and crosses, all piled together in grotesque confusion, just as the peasant carver had left them—a room not to be entered suddenly, or without a hint of its contents.

Here we stay during the whole of our visit. The living is good, and the charges are the same as at an ordinary German inn; the charge that seems the highest for a mountain village, viz. one florin (1s. 8d.) for each bed, is regulated by tariff.

Our hostess—who has also obtained places for us in the theatre—tells us in the course of the evening that the crowd will be so great on Sunday that a second performance will be given on the Monday to accommodate those who have come long distances to see the play.

But where is the theatre? Where are the performers? And where, in this little scattered village, can several thousand people lay their heads?

"We make up twelve hundred beds for visitors, and as for the rest who arrive at night, they can sleep well on sacks in their waggons," is the answer to the last inquiry. And we learn, too, that hundreds of peasants will arrive during the night and leave again in the evening after the performance.

It is now nearly 9 o'clock as we stroll through the village. The moon is just appearing from behind the "Kobelalp" (a frowning peak surmounted by two white crosses, which towers several thousand feet above the valley), and its reflection glitters in a trout stream winding far away through pastures. The last flock of goats is being shuffled home, the lights are being put out in the cottages (the house which is pointed out to us as "where the Christus lives" is dark and still), and the whole aspect of the place is so rustic and peaceful that we, a party of seven, from Munich, of various nations and creeds, decline altogether to believe that this can be

the home of histrionic art, and that by any possibility several thousand people will collect here next Sunday. But it is time to retire for the night in this primitive village. The last house to close is our hostess's, and the last creatures to retire to rest are the swallows, who build their nests in the corridors and sleep on the bells.

Early on Saturday morning we go to see the theatre, having permission to make some sketches of the interior, the peasants all going to

THE THEATRE AT OBERAMMERGAU.

their work in the fields or in their carving-shops as usual. It is a large wooden building with seats for about 6000 persons, nearly all open to the sky. The outside is all of plain timber planking, without any attempt at decoration, and without—we are thankful to observe—any huge bills or placards pasted upon its walls. The stage, which is about 120 feet broad and 170 feet deep, is uncovered, excepting at the back, where the *tableaux vivants* are set. There is a drop-curtain to this inner stage, with a view of Jerusalem painted by some village artist, and above the proscenium are figures of Faith, Hope, and Charity, also of a pelican feeding its young; and behind the stage *real* mountains rise with a gentle slope, which might remind the Eastern traveller of the Mount of Olives. The large stage, which is upon the plan of the old Greek theatres, has a scenic representation of two houses, with balconies on each side of the proscenium—the one on the right hand belonging to Annas, and that on the left to Pilate; and further to the right and left are two openings leading up to the back of the stage representing streets in Jerusalem.[1] The seats for the audience are still wet with rain that has fallen during the night, a few only at the back being covered and reserved. The prices for the seats vary from 5*s.* to about 6*d.*

We spend the greater part of the day here making drawings of the theatre, and of the mountains beyond, which we can see above the stage and on either side. Two lines of poplar trees mark the spot where the theatre is erected every ten years, and throw long shadows across the stage. There is nothing to disturb us, or any one to be seen, but a few peasants who stroll

---

[1] The words "right" and "left" are used throughout this description, looking *towards* the stage.

in with their children to choose places for the next day, and one or two carpenters who are repairing the stage. One of these, we learn afterwards, was Joseph of Arimathea; and the tall quiet-looking working-man who comes in with some friends, and looks over our shoulder whilst we are at work, is no less a personage than Joseph Mair, who to-morrow will personate the Christ.

CHAPTER III.

AT OBERAMMERGAU.

NOTHING could be more extraordinary than the change that has come over Oberammergau in the few hours during which we have been in the theatre, or strolling about the neighbourhood. It is now nearly six o'clock on Saturday evening, the vesper bells are ringing from the church tower, and the crowd is coming at last.

On every road and pathway, and down every mountain-side, the people come streaming in; and down the valley, as far as the eye can see, long lines of "Stellwagen" and "Bauerwagen" are toiling up the hill. The village church is crowded with peasant-women in their curious dresses, with handkerchiefs tied round the head; whilst here and there the grey Tyrolese costume and feathered hats of the men are conspicuous. Let us stop to look at them as they come flocking in in such quaint attire.

To those who live in Munich, and spend—as so many residents do—part of every summer in the neighbouring mountains and lakes, the costumes that we have sketched will be familiar enough. Some are to be seen indeed on fête days in the streets of Munich, but it is only on occasions of this kind, or at village gatherings such as the *Kirchweih*—the anniversary of the dedication of a church to its patron saint—that the quaintest and oldest are to be seen. The ordinary Tyrolese hat we all know (some of us indeed wear it), but the high black cap, resembling a grenadier's bearskin, generally worn by married women, is a curious relic of old days;

and the stiff dark-brocaded dresses which deform the figure, and give to the youngest and most graceful a hard, wooden appearance (the skirts projecting as in the sad days of crinoline) have been handed down from mother to daughter for several generations. The prevailing colour of the peasant-women's dresses is black or dark stuff, relieved with a bright-coloured shawl over the shoulders, and a white handkerchief tied over the head.

But some of the prettiest figures amongst the arrivals are the young girls in semi-Swiss costume (such as we have sketched on page 61), with dark velvet bodices, white sleeves, and silver chains, and their hats ornamented with gold tassels and flowers. In the crowd of men who lounge about, we may see the old swallow-tailed coat, of the rough brown order peculiar to Ireland, but adorned with rows of real silver coins instead of buttons.

COSTUME OF THE BAVARIAN TYROL.

THE ARRIVALS.

The procession of peasants in their gay colours and white handkerchiefs, backed by the green of the valley, with wooden chalets scattered here and there, and the blue of distant mountains, forms a picture rare to see and not easy to record. The sun is shedding its last rays across the valley, and lights up a group of peasants standing in the churchyard on rising ground, and we can just hear through the crowded doorway the "*Ora pro nobis*" and the tinkle of a silver bell.

But the plot thickens. Of such a crowd as flock in during the next few hours, and almost overwhelm the little village, it is difficult to give any idea in these pages; and how they disperse and disappear for the night is as extraordinary as the perfect order and method with which everything is done. The watchman cries the hours all through the Saturday night, but there cannot be many sleepers; and as he goes his rounds through the crowd of tent-like waggons that line the streets, it is like the patrol through a camp on the night before a battle.[1]

Soon after daybreak the sound of cannon is heard in the village, whilst at the church there

---

[1] We, and the peasants of Oberammergau, little thought, on that summer night, that before many days were over, some of the best men amongst them would be fighting for "Fatherland."

EARLY MASS.

have been masses every hour since two o'clock in the morning.

At 5 o'clock the whole population is up and stirring. Nearly every peasant who has come down from the mountains during the night commences the day with an act of worship, and then joins the throng, which at 7 A.M. renders the principal street (if we may call it one) almost impassable.

From the windows of the Langs' house the sight is extraordinary and impressive—on every side, both far and near, the people all tend one way.

> "For once all men seem one way drawn,
> See nothing else, hear nothing "—

and, judging from their faces, they are all of one mind, and are all bent upon a serious errand. Amongst the crowd that passes the door, it is easy to distinguish many who must be performers in the *Passionsspiel;* the ordinary grey costume of the men begins to have an Oriental tinge, and we see women and little children hurrying forward with gay costumes on their arms, and others bearing spears and banners, and (what would be called in theatrical parlance) the "properties" of the play; but all are quiet, orderly, and undemonstrative.

In front of our window, as we write these lines, a tall, dignified-looking man, of singularly modest demeanour, in working dress, with long flowing hair over his shoulders, stops for a moment to explain about some wood-carving which he is engaged upon for one of our party; this is Joseph Mair (the "Christus"), whom we saw yesterday in the theatre. Judas has just gone by — a quiet, amiable-looking man with nothing of the traitor about him—walking with Annas and Joseph of Arimathea. They follow so quickly that it is difficult to identify them all at the moment, but the group that is collecting

A SKETCH IN THE VILLAGE.

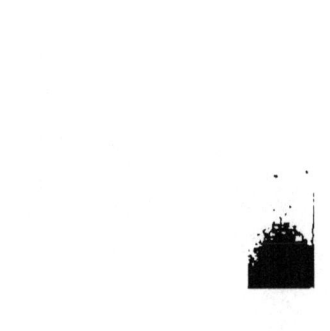

round our own door is perhaps the most interesting. There is Tobias Flunger (Pontius Pilate), who took the part of the "Christus" in 1850, his face as "refined, gentle, and dreamy now as when the shadow of the cross still lay upon it." Hand-in-hand with him is his daughter (the "Maria") talking with Peter; and by their side, chatting with our hostess's little daughters, is the beautiful Josepha Flunger, whose portrait is engraved on our frontispiece, and whom we shall presently see in the chorus in her classic robes, a model of statuesque grace. She is the leading contralto, the principal figure amongst the "peasant angels," who form the poetical exponents of the drama, and, as in the Greek theatre, point the moral of the play.

These peasants are so quiet, modest, and unassuming in manner that it is difficult to realise that they are actors; they have a word and a welcome for all, and with their frank manner and bright, healthy faces form a curious contrast to most actors—not one of the company whom we have seen this morning affects a portentous aspect, or is infected with stage gloom. They stay but a few minutes, and are quickly followed in the direction of the theatre by a crowd of minor performers, amongst whom are little children, some scarcely three years old, carried by their parents. Following them is the ass, with a rich covering, for the entry into Jerusalem; and lastly, a poor old man who personates Barabbas.

One word before entering the theatre. The costumes of the actors, and everything connected with the performance, show plainly that these villagers have spared no pains or expense in producing the play worthily; and it was but natural in this cynical age that they would be credited with mercenary motives in making the play attractive, with the intention of " making it pay," as the saying is. We believe we may say with truth that such suggestions would be unfair to the good people of Oberammergau. Joseph Mair himself is not a rich man, nor have any of the people amassed wealth by this means. In short—and this is the marvel of it—we witness at Oberammergau a whole population, from old men to children, agreed to do a noble act in a simple way.

CHAPTER IV.

THE PASSION PLAY.—PART I.

"How clearly on my inner sense is borne
The fair fresh beauty of the mountain morn,
And cries of flocks afar, and mixed with these
The green delightful tumult of the trees,—
The birds that o'er us from the upper day
Threw flitting shade, and went their airy way,—
The bright-robed chorus and the silent throng,
And that first burst and sanctity of song."[1]

E enter the theatre soon after 7 A.M., and find it already crowded with people, and by a quarter to eight there must be at least 5000 persons present,

---

[1] The beautiful idyll (in *Macmillan's Magazine* for August 1870) from which these lines are taken, strikes, to our mind, the truest chord in harmony with the *Passionsspiel*, of anything yet written.

nearly all of whom are of the peasant class. They are nearly all provided with the libretto, or book of the play, which is sold outside for a few pence; it is entitled, "The Great Atonement on Mount Golgotha; or the Sufferings and Death of Jesus." The text of the drama has been considerably altered and enlarged from time to time. At the beginning of the present century, it was almost rewritten by Ottmar Weis, one of the monks at the neighbouring monastery at Ettal, and the music was composed by Rochus Dedler, a native of the village; but before the performance of 1850 it was again altered and revised by Anton Daisenberg.

The events described are, with one exception, taken from the New Testament history of the Life and Death of Christ, commencing with his entry into Jerusalem. They are illustrated throughout by a series of prophetic *tableaux vivants*, taken from the Old Testament, and by the chorus, which explains, or accompanies, each scene and tableau with appropriate description or song.

At a few minutes before eight the orchestra, consisting of twenty-four performers—dressed in Tyrolese costume, with a leader wearing a straw hat—plays a short overture, when a gun is fired in the village, and the members of the chorus, twenty-one in number (nine men and twelve women), come filing slowly in from either side and take up their position in front of the stage thus.

. . . .

ORCHESTRA.

They are clad in robes of blue, mauve, and other bright colours, with white embroidered tunics and mantles of different colours; both men and women are dressed nearly alike, and are

JOHANN DIEMER (LEADER OF THE CHORUS).

arranged according to height, the men, with the leader of the chorus, standing in the centre. Johann Diemer, the leader, is differently attired from the rest; he has a white priestly robe, corded and embroidered with gold, and is the only one of the chorus that wears a beard. Josepha Flunger, the contralto, stands on the right hand, and takes a leading part in the choruses and descriptive music. They stand bareheaded in the sunlight, their fine bronzed features clearly distinguishable from every part of the theatre.

The *Chorführer*, or leader, first recites a prologue in a rich, clear voice, commencing with the solemn words:—

> "In holy wonder humbly bow,
> Oh race condemned!" &c.;

and the singers follow with explanatory verse (the music resembling one of Haydn's oratorios), raising their hands from time to time with natural, graceful gestures. And as they sing, they divide in the centre of the line and fall slowly back on either side, and the curtain rises on the *inner* stage, revealing a tableau of " Adam and Eve expelled from Paradise" by an angel with a flaming sword.[1] We see Adam and Eve standing side by side in the garden just as they are depicted to us in paintings, and an angel in a white robe, with a tinsel sword, driving them away. This first tableau was, artistically, a failure, and disappointed us greatly after all we had heard and read. But the second, representing "Angels bringing glad tidings upon earth," where we see a figure pointing to a cross, and women and children kneeling round it, and hear the chorus (also kneeling) singing in prophetic strain—

> " Lo ! from far on Calvary's heights
> A gleam of sunshine darkness lights "—

---

[1] Occasional reference to the drawing of the stage at page 48 will aid the reader in understanding these movements.

was much more impressive. The tableaux are shown for about three minutes, during which the figures, even of the little children, are literally as "motionless as statues." The sun shining upon the foremost figures, and upon the bare legs and feet of some of the performers, gives a curiously realistic effect.

As the curtain slowly falls, the singers close up in front of the large stage and continue their song in measured strains of thanksgiving, whilst the birds fly round them, and sing in the branches of the poplar trees which already begin to cast shadows across the stage.

After these two tableaux the actual play begins, consisting of seventeen scenes, commencing with "Christ's Entry into Jerusalem," and terminating with "the Ascension." The chorus slowly retires on either side, the inner curtain rises, and in the distance, winding down the narrow streets of Jerusalem, figures in Oriental costume appear flocking in on every side, singing, and waving palm branches in their hands; whilst the voices of the chorus are heard behind the scenes, singing—

> "All hail to thee, son of David—
> . . . . .
> Israel comes forth to greet thee!"

Gradually the figures crowd upon the immense open stage, the voices becoming louder, and the enthusiasm greater, every moment, when in the midst of the throng we see the Christ slowly riding down the street, closely followed by his apostles, and hemmed in on all sides by an eager, excited multitude, shouting, "Hosannas to the Son of David," throwing their garments on the ground, and singing songs of welcome.

The stillness of the immense audience at this moment was wonderful, and the whole effect was different from anything to be witnessed on the modern stage.[1] Every eye was turned towards the grand figure of Joseph Mair (the " Christus ") as he slowly dismounted from the ass and came into the midst of the crowd. It was as if the most pathetic picture of the Saviour that had ever been painted was moving before us; the noble figure, the sad, worn, dignified face (not the perfect ideal of da Vinci, but something, to our minds, much more human and touching), the dark flowing hair parted in the middle, the purple robe falling in the most perfect folds, the sandalled feet—all copied with strict fidelity from paintings by the old masters—every detail of costume, every attitude and gesture being rendered with accuracy, but, apparently, without

---

[1] A silence only disturbed by the wind through the trees; men being stationed outside at different points to prevent the approach of any one after the performance has commenced.

thought or care in the achievement. And here, as we are anxious to bring the portrait of the principal figure vividly before the reader, and as our engravings in some measure fail to do this, let us pause for a moment to relate the impressions of two other eye-witnesses, when they first "see the Christ."

"Joseph Mair is of an imposing presence, symmetrically built, with expressive features of an olive tint; his fine intellectual forehead rises over eyes full of a quiet melancholy, and the same serious, thoughtful, almost suffering expression is borne out by the entire cast of countenance, and by the delicately formed and fine lips, shaded by a pencilling of black moustache, and bordered by a wealth of beard that gives him a singular resemblance to the portrait of the Saviour by Rubens. His rich dark hair parted in the middle added to the illusion which was created by his entire look and gait—his

JOSEPH MAIR (THE "CHRISTUS").

extraordinary outward seeming of moderation, virtue, and self-denial."

Another description :—" From the moment that the procession wound on to the stage every interest centred in that strangely impressive figure, from which it was impossible to remove the eyes while it remained before them. The fear that there would hardly be enough majesty in the figure, or sufficient elevation, above personal mortification, to express the supernatural range of motive essential to the whole, disappeared in a moment. The singular grace of the purple robe did something; but Mair's complete possession by the radical idea of our Lord's life—an interior lived with the Father, which drew none of its deeper springs from mere earthly circumstance—gave to a dark face, and tender-speaking eyes, a grandeur of mien, and a complete "detachment" from all earthly passion which I have never seen in any of the painters' ideal Christs. For true and perfectly natural stateliness of movement and dignity of manner it was impossible to conceive Joseph Mair surpassed, realising to us in his manner and aspect the words of Christ to his apostles, 'Ye call me Master and Lord, and ye say well, for so I am.'"

The costume of the apostles, who stood behind the Christ, was also carefully portrayed; and it was easy to distinguish one from the other. There was Peter in a blue robe and yellow mantle, with bare feet, John in a red costume, and Judas in orange and yellow; all copied from the Italian masters, every fold of drapery being familiar to the eye as represented on canvas.

But the Jewish crowd had a more Oriental and picturesque colouring, and the variety of costume and attitude in the scene of the entry

JACOB HETT (PETER).

into Jerusalem formed a picture of the most effective kind; the number of persons on the stage must have been nearly three hundred, amongst whom were many little children, but there was scarcely one of that number who reminded the audience that they were witnessing a mimic scene.

The crowd welcomes Jesus of Nazareth, who comes "in the name of the Highest, to take possession of David's throne." Then appear the priests and Pharisees, the former in splendid robes, who confront the crowd, and turning to Jesus, ask, "Who art thou?" Jesus announces himself as the "Christ," and, passing on, goes up to the Temple (which we see at the back of the stage), and spreads consternation amongst the crowd assembled; and with the well-known words of Scripture, overturns the tables where the money-changers are sitting; the people retreat in haste, and some pigeons are seen to fly away above their heads.

The extraordinarily realistic character of this scene gave it a hold on the audience that nothing could exceed; from the beginning to the end there was nothing to remind one of the stage. The open-air effect, the spring foliage, the blue sky overhead, the singing of birds, and the rustling of wind through the trees, all added to the illusion; and the actors themselves, who were nearly all innocent of paint and powder, and who wore their own long hair and often had bare feet, had altogether—standing in the sun, and casting fitful shadows on the stage, their robes and hair blown about by the wind—an air of reality about them that it is impossible to convey to the reader in words. One and one only fault, as a picture, we had to find, viz. that some of the costumes, especially those of the apostles and of the chorus, being new this year, were too raw and modern-looking, and that occasionally mauve and magenta were introduced with an effect

PHARISÉE.

anything but pleasing to the eye. The scenery so far was sufficient, though not first-rate; but considering that everything was done by local artists, the result was wonderful. Two of the principal Munich actors, who had come to see the play for the first time, confessed that they had never seen such excellent acting; and the effect on the mind of the most critical and exacting of the audience was very remarkable.

The next tableau represents "Jacob's sons conspiring against Joseph," whilst the chorus, which has come again upon the stage, explains the type, and points the moral. This is followed by a scene showing the high court of the Sanhedrim (set at the back of the central stage), with Caiaphas, Annas, and other priests in council. They are clad in magnificent vestments, Caiaphas, whom we have sketched, being one of the most prominent. His dress was a long robe of rich crimson satin, embroidered with gold, and on his breast was an antique panel or breastplate, set with precious stones. His vest was white, embroidered with blue and purple, and on his head he wore a mitre, with the inscription, "Holiness to the Lord." The gorgeousness of these costumes was not more remarkable than their archæological accuracy and the Oriental flavour, if we may call it so, that pervaded every one of them.

The priests are seated at the farther end of the stage, with the rabbi in black robes, bound with cords of gold; and before them at two tables, the scribes, and, near the front on either side, Nicodemus and Joseph of Arimathea. The court are discussing with great animation what they shall do with Christ, when there enter suddenly on the scene the money-changers from the Temple, who make a formal accusation against him. Then the priests, one and all, pronounce vengeance " in the name of the God

JOHANN LANG (CAIAPHAS).

of Abraham, Isaac, and Jacob," and the curtain falls.

The sweet voices of the chorus, descriptive of the next two tableaux, will not be soon forgotten by those who heard them; and when they suddenly changed to a lament from the Song of Solomon, "Tell me, O ye daughters of Jerusalem," the effect was most sad and touching. The first of these tableaux represented "Tobias taking leave of his parents," and was remarkable for good grouping, and for a wonderful dog, which stood motionless for several minutes. In the second, "The Bride bewailing the loss of her husband" (which was one of the least successful of the tableaux), we see the bride surrounded by a group of maidens with flowers and musical instruments, whilst the chorus continue the lament—

> 'Where is he gone? O men and maidens, where
> Is gone the fairest amid all the fair?"
> * * * * * *

These tableaux introduce the scene of the journey to Bethany. Christ and his disciples come upon the stage, followed by Mary and Martha; they enter Simon's house, and it is here that Mary breaks the alabaster box of ointment and anoints the Christ. Judas protests against the waste, and is rebuked by the other disciples; then Christ takes leave of his mother, and they all depart.[1]

The next tableau represents "King Ahasverus on his throne, surrounded by his court." A magnificent and elaborate set scene, in which a crowd of figures is posed in the most skilful manner, the colours of the costumes contrasting and blending most effectively. Here the chorus

---

[1] There is little to say about the acting of the women; probably the necessity to strain the voice for such a vast audience gave them an air of effort and staginess from which nearly every one else was free. Their attitudes and costumes were like old pictures, but we heard little that they said. Mary, the mother of Christ, looked younger than her son.

FRANZISKA FLUNGER (THE "MARIA").

takes up the tale, and with explanatory verse tells
the meaning of the type, ending with the appeal,
"Jerusalem, Jerusalem, awake, and hear God's
word"; and it was in this as well as in several
succeeding tableaux that the action and impulse
of the chorus told with great dramatic power.
Every one is thus prepared for the scene which
follows; and when the curtain rises, and we see
in the distance the walls of Jerusalem, and Christ
and his disciples ascending the Mount of Olives,
we feel the full force of that never to be forgotten
lament over the "guilty city," and the pathos of
the words, "If thou hadst known, even thou, at
least in this thy day, the things which belong
unto thy peace!"

Peter and John now go forward to provide a
room for the Passover; Peter in his blue robe
and mantle of yellow—a fine bald-headed man,
the exact reproduction of familiar paintings; and
John, "the beloved disciple," a representative of

the commonly received ideal, both in face and appearance, of which the illustration on the opposite page gives a slight idea.

Next we see Judas, tempted to betray his Master. The acting of Lechner in this scene was admirable, and terribly true to nature, and there was a grim eccentricity about him that was both quaint and startling; his nervous attitude of restless musing, clutching at his yellow robes, his sudden start when touched upon the shoulder by one of his tempters, the conflicting emotions of greed, fear, and sorrow all passing through his mind, touched the audience with feelings that they could scarcely suppress. So wonderful was the power with which this character was portrayed, and so sad the picture of poor human nature given over to evil, that the audience could hardly restrain from open expressions of sympathy and sorrow for his sin. But it was the actor's power, more than anything in the dialogue,

JOHANNES ZWINK (JOHN), AGED 19.

that moved them thus; be it right or wrong, we must record the fact that Judas throughout the play excited an interest and sympathy second only to the "Christus."

In the following tableau, the inner stage was crowded with the "Israelites receiving manna from heaven"; and was one of the best we had yet seen. The attitudes of the little children in the foreground, some lying on the ground, others with hands upraised, were wonderful for the training displayed, giving a fixed, wax-work effect to the group. The massing of colour was a study in itself.

The curtain falls for a moment, when the same figures are seen again, in different attitudes, and in the centre, an enormous bunch of grapes borne on a pole between two men. Moses and Aaron are conspicuous in both these tableaux—Moses in a red robe, Aaron in white; they point to the fruit that comes from Jordan, whilst the chorus explains the prophetic meaning of the two tableaux, viz. the bread and wine at the Last Supper.

The celebration of the Passover, which immediately follows, is copied from the celebrated fresco by Leonardo da Vinci, and was one of the most solemn and remarkable scenes in the play; the acting of Joseph Mair, as the Christ, was admirable for its quiet tone, and its extraordinary dignity and grace. When the curtain drew up, and Christ and his apostles were seen seated at the table, and Joseph Mair rose to administer the sacrament, one or two of the audience near us abruptly left the theatre; and when—to use the words of another writer—"Christ took off his mantle, and wrapped a towel around his waist, in order to go round and wash the feet of his apostles, there was just one suppressed laugh of derision. But the peasantry saw nothing ridiculous in it, neither did the more educated part of the audience. During the progress of the Christ from one to another with his calmly earnest features—sad as if presaging his agony—a strain of soft music broke tremulously in waves of sound from the back of the stage. The bread was broken and distributed, and the wine filled into the goblet, exactly as recorded in the Scriptures, and John (who sat beside him and leaned upon his Master), asking Christ who would betray him, was answered, 'He it is, to whom I shall give a sop, when I have dipped it'; and when the sop was given to Judas with the words, 'That thou doest, do quickly,' the traitor started up with fierce hyena-like eyes and rushed from the room."

The exit of Judas and the perplexed and alarmed attitude of the other apostles—

"A gaze that half was horror, half was awe"—

were represented in the most natural manner, amid the breathless attention of the people.

Soon after this, Christ gives his apostles his final command, and they all go together to the garden of Gethsemane.

In the tableau which follows, Joseph is represented being sold by his brethren for twenty pieces of silver, whilst the singers again explain its prophetic meaning, and denounce Judas as "the betrayer of his Lord"; and as they sing, the curtain rises, and we see the hall of the Sanhedrim, with Caiaphas and the chief priests assembled in council. Judas is brought before them, and after much hesitation and debate, he agrees for a price to betray his Master. Here again the acting of Lechner was painfully real; his temptation and final acceptance of the bribe, the nervous, eager counting out of the money on a table before the council, the grasping of a coin that rolled away from the heap, and his retreat with the bag that held "the price of blood," excited the audience to almost the only

GREGOR LECHNER.

outward expression or manifestation during the day. The half smothered word "Judas" was perpetually on the lips of the audience, and he seemed (as we hinted before) to excite something almost akin to sympathy amongst the spectators. In this scene Joseph of Arimathea and Nicodemus address the assembled council, and protest against the injustice of the proceedings, but their voices are of no avail against the universal verdict, "Let him die!"

After this scene follow three tableaux representing respectively, "Adam toiling in the fields"; "Joab, captain of the host of David, kissing Amasa, and stabbing him with the right hand"; and "Samson overwhelming the Philistines"; which the chorus explains as typical of the agony of Christ in the garden, the betrayal with a kiss, and the final triumph of Christ over his enemies. The second of these tableaux was remarkable for the graceful *pose* of the two principal figures, and for the grand apostrophe, by the chorus, to the "Rock of Gibeon"; but some of the scenery and details of these as in former tableaux were, we are bound to record, very poor and inartistic.

Following these are, first, "The Agony in the Garden," a very trying and difficult scene, admirably acted by Joseph Mair, but marred in effect by the lowering of a stage angel; next, "The Betrayal"; "The attack on Malchus by Peter"; and "The healing of the wound by a touch."

> "Thro' all these scenes the fateful story ran,—
> * * * *
> There was the evening feast, remembered long,
> The mystic act and sacramental song;
> There was the dreadful garden, rock and tree,
> Waker and sleeper in Gethsemane."
> * * * *

Finally we see Christ deserted by his disciples and led away.

Thus ends the first half of the play (in which there are seven scenes and eleven tableaux), which has lasted without intermission for nearly four hours, without a single hitch or sign of hesitation on the part of the performers, great or small. It is nearly twelve o'clock, and the members of the chorus, who have stood bareheaded in the sun nearly all the time, must have need of rest. In ten minutes the theatre is almost deserted, and the village is alive with people.

Sudden as the change was, it was a relief to be again in the open fields, and to come back to common life. What that life was immediately outside the theatre, and what a change had come over the spirit of the scene, a more skilful pen than ours shall tell. "The bells rang, the peasants refreshed themselves beneath the trees in gay groups, or crowded into the village inn. And what a bustle there was in that little inn! In the lower rooms, a devouring of food and a swallowing of beer; a cloud of smoke, and a noise of tongues. In the gardens and in front of the houses, rows of gaily attired peasants seated at long tables drinking beer out of quaintly shaped glasses with pewter lids; trees waving above their heads, roses and lilies blooming around them, a background of Tyrolean roofs, covered with large round stones; and sharp jagged Alpine peaks rising closely behind the chalets into the sunny sky."

A pleasant stream (the Amber) flows through the village, and as we follow its windings down the valley away from this noisy crowd (passing a little *Bierhaus* on the way where priests, Pharisees, and Roman soldiers are busy at their midday meal, and a horse caparisoned for a procession in a future scene is quietly grazing by their side), we see at a little distance a figure seated on the ground, whose features are strangely familiar—it is Judas, calmly smoking a pipe on the river's brink.

CHAPTER V.

*"Oh how hard a task, to set again
The living Christ among the homes of men!"*

THE PASSION PLAY.—PART II.

AT half past twelve a gun is fired in the village, and in a few minutes the theatre is again filled with people. The sun is now burning upon the sea of heads between us and the immense open stage; a sea, as Anna Howitt describes it, "whose waves were Tyrolean hats and glittering *Ringelhaube*, tipped by white handkerchiefs like a dash of foam."

Again the chorus comes filing in, and sings the sad refrain that sounds so mournfully through the trees. The wind has risen, and their bright robes are tossed into wide horizontal folds, and the dark tresses of Josepha Flunger are streaming in the wind. There is the same stillness and awe, the same unwearied aspect and solemn expression on the bronzed faces of the peasants, which makes the confusion of the last hour (harmless as it was) seem, by contrast, dreadful and almost impossible.

The second part opens with a striking tableau, showing Ahab and Jehoshaphat, the kings of Israel and Judah, seated on thrones; and before them Micaiah, the prophet of the Lord, smitten on the cheek by Zedekiah—a type, as the chorus explains, of Christ brought before Annas and Caiaphas. The effective grouping and arrangement of colour in this tableau were most remarkable, considering the small space in the inner stage, and the number of figures massed together. When the chorus retires, immediately there enters a crowd of people bringing Christ before Annas, who appears on the balcony of his house. The exciting nature of this scene (also of the following one before Caiaphas) and the natural manner in which all, even the little children in the crowd, bore their parts, could not be imagined, nor can we easily picture them to the reader. The attitude of Joseph Mair as the Christ standing in the midst of the mocking crowd, his appeal to Annas (answered by a blow), brought tears to many eyes; and when Judas comes in eager haste to announce his success, and Annas replies to him, "Your name shall live for ever," the dramatic effect was perfect. Nothing that action could do was wanting to give the idea of isolation and solitary grandeur on the part of the principal character, and the result was really sublime. Whatever differences of opinion we, spectators, may have had as to the acting of Joseph Mair, we were all in accord during this scene.

After two more tableaux—one representing

"the stoning of Naboth," and another of Job, poor and in misery, seated by a well, his wife mocking him and telling him to " curse God and die "— Christ is brought in bound before Caiaphas, the soldiers treating him roughly, and the crowd laughing him to scorn. Here, again, the tall figure of the Christ towering above his persecutors, and the (apparently unconscious) statuesque attitude in which he stood, aided by the simple folds of his drapery—composed, if we may use the word, so as to form an admirable study for painter or sculptor.

Christ is next led into a hall in the house of Caiaphas, where he is again accused; a scribe reads the law, and Christ is finally condemned and taken away to be arraigned before Pilate.

All this time Peter and John, who have followed their Master, have been seen amongst the crowd; Peter, now subdued and cowed, passes through an outer hall where the soldiers are

RABBI.

seated round a fire, and a woman at once recognises him as one of the followers of Christ. He denies it, and as he does so the third time, a cock crows, and Christ is brought in surrounded by soldiers and guards. He looks on Peter, who goes out full of sorrow; and Christ, after being cruelly treated, spat upon, and knocked down by the soldiers, is led away.

The "Murder of Abel" is the next tableau, in which the remorse of Cain is exhibited as the awful punishment for sin, in this world and the next; a refined and striking contrast, it may here be observed, to the practice in old times in these plays of typifying the remorse of Judas. When the curtain draws up, we see the hall of the Sanhedrim again, where Caiaphas and the chief priests are seated in council; and Judas, in his orange and yellow robes, his hair blown about by the wind, flitting to and fro on the stage, clutching at his bag, the price of blood! Nothing seemed to move the audience more than this terrible figure, when, in an agony of remorse, he rushes into the midst of the council, and—unable to turn them from their purpose—throws down the bag of silver and with a wild shriek of despair flies from the city. The tragic effect of this scene, on those, if there were any, who were able to regard it as they would an ordinary drama, was extraordinary; and in the following one, where we see him in the last act of desperation, unloosing his girdle, and climbing a tree as the curtain falls, a woman in the audience fainted.

The tableau of " Daniel before Darius " precedes the next scene, where Christ is brought before Pilate, who comes out on the balcony of his house on the left of the stage. Here the question is put by Caiaphas, " Art thou the Christ?" and the answer is quietly given, " Thou sayest it." Two soldiers are then sent down into

TOBIAS FLUNGER (PILATE).

the street, and Christ is brought up on to the balcony of Pilate's house, to be questioned. Pilate finally refers the multitude to Herod, and Christ is led away.

In the next scene (preceded by a tableau of "Samson in the temple of Dagon"), we see Herod seated on his throne, and Christ brought bound before him. Herod interrogates Christ, who answers not a word, and is finally given up to the people. The soldiers array him in a long cloak; whilst the people cry aloud, "Let him die!" and the curtain falls again. Then follow two tableaux—"Joseph's brethren showing Jacob the coat of many colours," and "Abraham about to sacrifice Isaac"—inferior pictures, it must be owned, to many that had preceded them, but remarkable for the fine effect of the music which, through all these scenes, carries the story on with unflagging interest; the chorus pointing the moral of each separate tableau, and keeping our attention fixed on the scenes one by one, which (whatever be the effect on the reader of this narrative) never seemed wearisome to those who witnessed them.

There was no rest for those who acted, and none for those who looked on. The curtain had no sooner fallen on these two tableaux—typical, as will be understood, of the great sacrifice— when shouts of "He ought to die!" heralded the approach of an excited crowd before Pilate's house, and Christ is brought out and stripped, and scourged by the soldiers. They put upon him a scarlet robe and a reed in his hand, and mockingly hail him as "King of the Jews"; then they strip him and bind him to a pillar (as in the illustration), and put a crown of thorns upon his head, pressing it on to his bruised forehead by means of two crossed sticks, and then the curtain falls before the fainting, suffering Christ. "This passage from the 'Passion,'" writes one who

JOSEPH MAIR (THE "CHRISTUS").

witnessed it, " is set before us with a grim literalness that makes women and the tender-hearted shut their eyes. But (and this is what seemed to strike us all during this scene) never have I had such a conception of what Christ must have suffered, as this piece of pre-Raphaelistic acting realised to my mind. The limbs of the Christ, looking like marble, formed one of those rare studies of the human form which startle us by their beauty."

The complete passiveness of the Christ in the hands of the soldiers, as they struck and insulted him, were all accompanied by a look, not of fortitude and tension, but rather of what the Roman Catholics call "recollection"—a look as if there was nothing in their coarse questions and insults to which any genuine answer, explanation, or expostulation, were appropriate. Nothing struck me more forcibly than the effect of this prolonged, and hardly broken, silence of the Christ. In *reading* the history, one cannot realise this, both because the events pass far too quickly in the terse narrative, and because such silence, till you *see* it, is a negative and not a positive conception.

Two more tableaux, the first a magnificent one, of "Joseph honoured by the Egyptians," riding in a chariot surrounded by a dense crowd of people assembled to do him honour; and the second, "the Scapegoat." Here the chorus explains with great solemnity, the type of One who "bore the sins of the world upon him"; and as they sing, the shouting of the populace is heard without, and the terrible words, "An's Kreuz mit ihm! an's Kreuz mit ihm! Sein Blut komme über uns und unsere Kinder!" (in a curious local dialect, which gave, if anything, a greater realism to the scene), are echoed through the streets of the city.[1] Soon the stage

---

[1] It is necessary to the adequate conception of these scenes to bear in mind that the sides of the proscenium—representing

is filled with an angry, excited multitude, calling upon Pilate to put Christ to death, and to release to them Barabbas. Pilate appears on the balcony of his house, and Christ stands immediately beneath it. Caiaphas and the chief priests are ranged on the left, and on the right the Jewish crowd. This scene, which is one of the finest in the play, was acted with great ability by Tobias Flunger as Pilate, and as a picture was beautiful, both in colour and grouping. The figure of the Christ standing before his accusers, the crowd clamouring for his death—the same crowd, the same little children, who but a short time since sang Hosannas in his honour, and spread palm branches in his path, now shout and

---

streets in Jerusalem, which reach to the back of the stage— are *always* open to the spectator; and that figures are often seen in the distance, and voices heard, when the central curtain is down. This arrangement affords facilities for effects superior to anything on an ordinary stage.

scream for his blood! Pilate orders a vessel of water to be brought in, and, washing his hands, says, "I am guiltless of the blood of this just person." The people shout in reckless, revengeful haste, "His blood be on us and our children"; throwing up their arms, and pressing forward until restrained by the Roman guard.

Then at last Barabbas is brought forward, looking grim and dazed, clad in a coarse brown prison dress, with bare feet and matted locks. They stand side by side, the beautiful statuesque figure of the Christ, his hands bound behind him, and the wretched Barabbas. Pilate makes one final appeal to the people; but it is of no avail, Barabbas is their choice, and he is led joyfully away.

The end of the drama now draws near. After two tableaux—"Abraham and Isaac going up Mount Moriah, with wood for sacrifice," and

JOHANN ALLINGER (BARABBAS).

"Moses showing the people in the wilderness the brazen serpent," which the chorus explains as the type of the Cross to which all must look to be saved—a great multitude is seen to emerge from the gates of Jerusalem, with Christ bearing the cross on his way to Calvary. The procession, with guards on foot and on horseback, winds down the street on the right of the spectator, and as it turns to ascend the Via Dolorosa, they meet Simon, who is roughly seized, and made to bear the cross. It is here that Christ sees his mother approaching, accompanied by Mary Magdalene and John, the beloved disciple; he stops to address them, and then follows the touching appeal to the daughters of Jerusalem, which brings tears to many eyes.

An incident is here introduced, almost the only one not to be found in the Gospel narrative, that of St. Veronica offering the handkerchief to our Lord; but the action harmonised so completely with the rest of the scene that we hardly noticed the innovation.

Soon they pass on, and as the long procession winds up the Mount of Calvary, the curtain falls, and the chorus re-enters, clad in black cloaks, with black wreaths and crosses on their foreheads. They address the audience, and sing—in minor music, accompanied by harps and stringed instruments—a long lament urging all men to "weep and bewail, for the Lord is gone." Here, strange to relate, the sky becomes overcast, and the mountains are hidden in a cloud of mist.[1] There is a muffled sound of hammering on a cross, and suppressed sobs are heard from the people, when the curtain rises, and the great scene of the Crucifixion is before us. In the centre the Christ, fastened to the cross, is lying on the

---

[1] For fear that this may be thought fanciful, we may mention that the *Times* correspondent and other newspaper writers record the same incident.

ground, and on either side the two thieves, already raised, are hanging, bound with cords. The soldiers slowly raise the central figure into its position, which reaches nearly to the top of the proscenium, the crowd falls back, and we see a *living* Christ upon the cross!

It matters not to the spectators *how* the beautiful form of the Christ is suspended (though the means are no secret), so that every limb should fall into the most perfect lines.[1] It is enough for us to record that every detail of the Gospel narratives is brought realistically before us: we see the suffering figure, the torn and bleeding

---

[1] Joseph Mair was suspended on the cross for twenty minutes. He was supported by a concealed band round the waist, iron clamps for the hands, and a rest for the left foot. The physical exertion in this position was much greater than would appear from a distance. The perfect pose of his figure, copied from well-known paintings of the crucifixion, actually exceeded them in beauty. The light flesh-coloured dress he wore refined the outline and heightened the effect.

hands, and the bruised head with the crown of thorns. Everything is carried out to the letter, even to the piercing of the side with a spear and the breaking of the legs of the thieves. The soldiers on the ground tear up Christ's garments, and throw dice to "cast lots for his vesture." Every incident is depicted with terrible reality, and when the end comes, when the Saviour utters the final words, "It is finished!" when darkness ensues and a crash of thunder follows (the more startling from the deep silence of the spectators), and a messenger comes rushing breathless on the stage to announce to the awe-stricken crowd that "the veil of the temple is rent in twain"— the climax of tragedy is reached.

The effect on the audience at this moment was perhaps the most impressive and fearful ever witnessed in a theatre. The poor peasants, men and women, gave way under the strain, and wept aloud; and even those who could look upon it as upon an ordinary drama, held their breath. There was (apparently) not one mocking spirit amongst five thousand people, or one human soul the worse for being present that day.

Everything that follows seems to the spectator an anti-climax; but we must follow the story to the end. Joseph of Arimathea and Nicodemus come to take down the body of Christ. They bring long ladders, and Nicodemus, ascending behind the figure, passes a long band of new linen cloth under the arms of the body of Christ, and then proceeds, with much apparent difficulty, to take out the nails and lower the body from the cross. At this point, when Mary, his mother, steps forward to prevent the soldiers from touching the body of Christ, we are reminded of paintings so familiar to us that the living copy is startling. All three figures are finally lowered, the limbs falling one by one as they are released, with an effect almost too death-like and terrible. It will not be surprising to learn that here one or two women fainted, and that several had to leave the theatre.

Those who were near the stage amongst the peasants (as we were on the second day) could judge better of the care with which every little detail was carried out, until it was almost *too painful;* we could see that the central figure was covered (as it appeared) with drops of blood from the crown of thorns, and that the hands and feet were torn and injured with the great nails that Nicodemus drew out with difficulty and threw down. These things were horrible to witness, but not more horrible than the thousands of miserable wooden images of the Saviour, before which this peasant community is accustomed to bow down.

It would be well for the reader, and for the spectator, if the history of the *Passionsspiel* closed at this scene, which could not have been represented more perfectly, or with more reverent regard for the Scripture narratives.

The two succeeding tableaux were weak in comparison with what had gone before; the first, "Jonah and the whale," was ludicrous, and "the destruction of the Egyptians in the Red Sea," with Pharaoh's host struggling with stage waves, would have been better omitted; but the chorus—(never wearying through the long day and who now re-entered in bright robes)— redeemed these artistic failures with their joyful strains. Their faces were raised to the sky, and their voices came trembling on the breeze in uncertain waves of sound—strains that resounded through the hills, telling of the "greatness and goodness of the Lord!"

In the last scene we see the tomb, set at the back of the inner stage, and the Roman soldiers watching without. There is a noise as of an earthquake, the stones of the tomb fall away, and Christ is seen for a moment at the door. Mary Magdalene comes to the tomb, and an angel appears to her, and tells her that "He is risen." Then come Caiaphas and the priests and soldiers, who soon depart in dismay. Peter and John approach, with Mary Magdalene, saying, "They have taken away my Lord, and I know not where they have laid him." The risen Christ appears to her again, and the curtain falls.

One final tableau—representing "Christ surrounded by saints in glory," accompanied by the beautiful Hallelujah chorus of the "peasant angels" of Oberammergau—ends the play; and, for the first time during the day, the audience give vent to their pent-up feelings by a burst of applause, which echoes amongst the hills.

CHAPTER VI.

THE AUDIENCE AND THE ACTORS.

T was not the least curious or interesting experience of these eventful days to notice the various types of character that the great play had brought together, and to remark the effect (as far as appeared on the surface) on the minds of the audience. The earnest attention and endurance of this vast congregation (we use the word in its literal sense) strike every visitor, but it is only by going amongst the peasants that we can fully comprehend its effect upon them. Let us take a leaf out of our note-book just as we wrote it down in the afternoon of Monday, the second day.

"It is now nearly four o'clock in the afternoon, and the figures that we have sketched from different points in the theatre have, most of them, sat in the sun since seven in the morning, with only a short interval of rest, and we could have wished that some who have considered it their duty to denounce the 'miracle play' from pulpits in England and elsewhere, were here to see how the people conduct themselves through the day. These peasants have one obvious advantage over an ordinary congregation, that, wearing a national, *unchanging* costume, their attention is not diverted to the exciting study of some 'new fashion'; they have nothing to do or to attend to, for seven hours, but the

A SKETCH IN THE THEATRE

business that they have come upon; and they do it with their whole heart."

But, although the general effect of the play on the peasant audience was undoubtedly good, and from what we could judge—after witnessing two performances from every part of the theatre—to the majority most impressive, it was not regarded by them entirely as a religious ceremony. The peasants had more the attitude of being in a picture gallery; they were more or less impressed, but evidently under no particular restraint of conduct. Some were in tears, and one or two indeed hysterical towards the end; and some—let us be exact—took beer frequently through the day. They came and went as they pleased, they brought their little children, and old men were carried in and had every incident read to them from the book of the play.

This was the aspect of it, and for the audience for whom it was intended, the teaching was undoubtedly good. To those to whom religion is taught by outward impressions, it was a picture speaking to them in a language they could understand of a religion already imprinted upon their hearts; and (to use the words of one of their own people) "of all the pictures of the sufferings and passion of Christ we have ever seen, this is the most beautiful and the best."[1]

The ordinary tourist or visitor, attracted by curiosity, will contemplate the play with mixed feelings, according to his education or religion,

---

[1] We have been asked, nay, urged, in publishing this account of the *Passionsspiel*, to omit any details that would detract from its solemn aspect, or any description that might appear flippant or irreverent in the telling. It is impossible to draw the line, but we may add that there were many odd scenes, and even ludicrous incidents, inseparable from a theatrical performance in which nearly 400 people were engaged, which those who, like ourselves, were behind the scenes during part of one day, were obliged to witness, but which have been omitted in this narrative because it would have been unfair to write them down.

but the effect upon all, when we were present, was solemn to an extraordinary degree; there was little to shock the most sensitive religious instincts, and little for the most critical to disapprove of. There were some realistic parts of the play, such as the Crucifixion scene and the breaking the legs of the thieves on the cross, which some women had better not see; and one or two of the tableaux, such as Jonah and the whale, would have been better omitted; but the general effect was so solemn and grand that, if it were possible to divest the play of all religious interest, and to contemplate it simply as a well-acted tragedy, it would fix the attention of an audience fresh from the theatres of London or Paris. This we say without an irreverent thought, to give the reader the best idea of its merits as a dramatic performance.

In speaking thus far of the effect of the play on the minds of the audience, it may be thought that we are recording first impressions, and that a calmer judgment will condemn all religious dramatic representations. Does it, or does it not?

What does an Italian priest (who has crossed

the Alps to witness the *Passionsspiel*), now walking in his cloistered garden on the hills above Verona, think of these things? What does he, who has denounced, and even tried to suppress, these plays, say now after months of reflection? He has but one answer to the question, an answer eloquent and expressive enough, he has—"*seen the Christ!*"

What does this drama teach little children, whose imagination is filled with figures of blue and yellow saints—who start in their dreams at hideous images of a bleeding Saviour, which their "mother church" is ever holding before their eyes?

What does one Englishwoman write home? "The simple grandeur of the 'Christus' was almost awful; I forgot all but the wonderful story of our salvation, and cried all day."

There was one figure sitting near us during the day, a well-known face and a well-known name in London society, whose customary place at that hour in the afternoon was the bow window of a Westend club, who was literally "bathed in tears."

What are we to think of these things, and

what shall we say, when the *Times* correspondent writes, " I have never seen so affecting a spectacle, or one more calculated to draw out the best and purest feelings of the heart "?

But (and because nothing we can ever say will persuade some readers that the *Passionsspiel* at Oberammergau is a good and right thing to do) let us not trust to individual impressions, but rather record the truth gathered from various sources, that to many Christian minds the fact of having *seen* the events recorded in Gospel narrative pass before their eyes, has done more to impress the Scripture narrative upon them than a life of teaching.

Those who are familiar with the records of the religious plays in the middle ages—who remember that in our own cathedrals of Chester and Coventry "Mystery Plays" and "Moralities" of the coarsest, and most irreverent kind were exhibited with the sanction of the Church—may not be disposed to listen with favour to this narrative.

But the *Passionsspiel* at Oberammergau is as different from the miracle play called the "Harrowing of Hell," performed in England in the reign of Edward II., as the noblest tragedy from the commonest farce; and there is, as may have been gathered from the foregoing, a protestant simplicity about the entire performance which is strangely at variance with Roman Catholic teaching.[1] It was generally remarked at Oberammergau, that the Virgin Mary seldom appeared in the play, that Peter's most prominent act was the denial of his Lord, and that there was an adherence to facts in the Scripture

---

[1] It has been suggested, with some reason, that the most realistic scenes in the *Passionsspiel* are so reverently and carefully portrayed—and are, moreover, so familiar to most of us in paintings—that they are divested of half their painfulness to the spectator.

narrative almost without precedent in the records of these plays.

But without going further into the history of miracle plays — of which the one at Oberammergau is almost the only relic—we would repeat that all those of which we read in former times lacked the finish and conscientious care bestowed upon this performance.

The year 1870 was probably the culminating point of excellence at Oberammergau, for the reason that the performers still retained their simplicity of character, combined with an amount of artistic excellence never before achieved; in 1880 it may be otherwise, the sons and daughters of these peasants are being educated in cities, and will bring back with them too much knowledge of the world.[1]

---

[1] They may learn to read English, and to teach their children on a plan lately advocated in one of our newspapers. "I have

RELIGIOUS PLAYS.

However—and this seems to be the great argument for the decennial reproduction of the *Passionsspiel*—as it is the universal fate of Christian men to be surrounded, not only in their homes, but wherever they congregate, by *bad* pictures of Gospel history, we should be thankful to the peasants of Oberammergau for

---

a Noah's ark," writes a correspondent of the *Nonconformist*; "and with bricks and animals we illustrate Scripture narratives. Last Sunday evening we had Rahab letting the spies down from the wall. The building of Jericho was a serious work. My construction was Rahab's house on the wall, and the spies in the act of descending in a basket, improvised of card-board. Next Sunday we shall have the disciples in the Lake of Galilee. The table-cloth will form the water, and will be arranged for the occasion in waves. Round about with the bricks we shall make the shore, putting Nazareth and other towns in their proper situations. A joiner will soon make you the bricks of elm or ash. Noah's arks are cheap; and you will find in the very heart of the play many unexpected opportunities of fixing Scripture narratives, and their spiritual lessons, on the children's minds!

their beautiful and simple method of religious teaching.

Let us add a few words about the acting, judged by the ordinary standards of criticism. The rendering of the principal characters was, as may be gathered from the foregoing, something quite unique and remarkable. They never turned towards, or appealed to, the audience; they seldom walked with a stage stride; they never kept the "stage waiting," as the saying is, and even the little children never took a wrong position or attitude: they were nearly always *natural*, and nearly always *right*.

Joseph Mair was a wonderful instance of simplicity of manner, and few men could have been physically better suited for the part. His face, with which many will be disappointed in our large engraving, was not the ordinary, received, type of beauty; but in the latter scenes of sorrow and suffering nothing could have been better. His tall, imposing figure, upon which the robes fell in such graceful lines, the wonderfully beautiful modelling of his limbs on the cross, his action during the delivery of the dialogue, were more impressive and effective, from a dramatic point of view, than anything we have seen on the modern stage. If we say that the delivery of some of the sentences was slightly monotonous, we have mentioned the only fault in an otherwise perfect performance. How he arrived at this perfection, will naturally be asked. The answer is that he had studied the part for years, and was thoroughly imbued with the character, and entered into its personation heart and soul. He was proud of the achievement, but in the most simple-hearted way; he felt it an honour and a privilege to have this part, and he performed it as he would carve the figure of the Saviour in wood in his workshop, *con amore*, and with reverence and fear. But—and this is perhaps the key to the mystery—*he would not excel in acting, or carving, anything else.*

There was some difference of opinion as to Mair's elocution, one being of opinion that the "tone and voice were far below the acting, and that, when he spoke, he broke that wonderful spell that bound everybody." We should think that, excepting as we said, being slightly monotonous, he was as nearly perfect as it was possible. There was little trace of a Bavarian accent, and no slurring over words or making "points"; if anything, he was too measured and careful. Some of the apostles had just that local flavour about their speech which would become Galileans, whose "speech bewrayed them" in the capital.

Next to Joseph Mair, the acting of Gregor Lechner, as Judas, was the most complete. It was remarkable for the breadth and unflagging energy with which so difficult a part was sustained. In his case he could not identify himself as closely with the character, and more was required of the actor; and yet the reader will have seen in the course of the play that he was both natural and effective. Here, again, the continual rehearsals mentioned in the first chapter, and the system adopted at Oberammergau of selecting each actor to the part for which he seemed best fitted, assisted greatly to this result. But the statement which appeared in some newspapers, that "the assignment of the parts of Judas or Barabbas to any members of the community was equivalent 'to a black mark,' and indicated more than equivocal character," was an unintentional libel upon some most worthy men—a libel that we had the authority of the actors themselves to contradict.[1] The portrait of Judas at page 103

---

[1] Referring to this report, one of the villagers quaintly remarked that "it would be difficult to find a bad man who could act so well!"

is (as any one who saw the performance in 1870 will attest) an admirable likeness, and the type of face could hardly, we think, have been better chosen.

Peter and John were the exact reproductions of paintings and church windows; they were perpetually falling into what we should call "stained-glass attitudes," and their studied accuracy of demeanour was sometimes monotonous. A few of the characters were stagey. Caiaphas, for instance, was mannered, almost bombastic; and had a stage stride. The Maria also had an appearance of effort and constraint. Some of the minor parts, such as that of Barabbas, were admirably sustained, and what is called the "stage business" was always effective. The counting out of the thirty pieces of silver to Judas, and the casting lots by the soldiers at the foot of the cross, were instances of this.

But to an artistic eye the arrangement and

grouping of the crowds on the stage, their attitudes when shouting a welcome, or crying out for revenge; the variety of their costumes, and the Eastern colouring given to most of the scenes, were more striking than any copies of Italian pictures. In the tableaux the massing of colour and the grouping of figures (though often too crowded on the inner stage) were most skilful, showing that a thoroughly artistic spirit was at work, and that each individual must have been imbued with it. There was a freedom of action evident everywhere, quite unusual on the ordinary stage; in the crowded tableaux it would have been impossible to set them in the time (two or three minutes), had not every one fallen of his own accord into his proper place and position.

The scenery, which was exposed continually to sun and rain, and was viewed without the assistance of footlights, or anything to aid the effect, was of course the least satisfactory part, but it was sufficient for the purpose, and wonderful considering the limited resources at command. The best scenes and most impressive groups were entirely independent of stage accessories.

CHAPTER VII.

"Where is he gone? O men and maidens, where
Is gone the fairest amid all the fair?
Mine eyes desire him, and with dawning day
My heart goes forth to find him on the way."

ANY were the tears shed in Oberammergau when early one July morning Joseph Mair, together with several of the performers, took leave of his people and went off to the wars.

Two hundred years ago this valley was devastated with pestilence, "caused by the drain of men absorbed in the wars of

Gustavus Adolphus, and the consequent poverty of the people"; and now, in the very year of its decennial celebration, war broke out again, and all the young men in Oberammergau had to join the army, and the play was stopped.

"We have just had the last performance of the *Passionsspiel*.[1] The 'Christus' has had to join the artillery; he had an interview with the king to beg to be allowed to retain his long hair, so that, when the war was over, he might be able to resume his part. The request was granted. None are left to gather in the harvest but old men, women, and children. It is heartbreaking to go amongst those left behind, and to feel that those we love best are gone to the war. One wakes in the morning feeling as if the whole thing was a hideous dream."

---

[1] Letter from Munich, July 1870.

The abrupt termination of the *Passionsspiel* in 1870 was to be regretted on many grounds, especially that many artists and actors, who were on the road at the time, and who " would not be persuaded" until they had seen the play with their own eyes, will never see it as well performed as recorded in these pages. As a work of art of the most effective kind, powerful and eloquent in its teaching, it could never be surpassed; and we who witnessed it could not help thinking of the effect this play might have had upon some students of art, if they had had time to come here before the war.

It would have taught them, we venture to say, at least one thing—that truth in art is the one thing needful to success, and earnestness in the work the battle half won; that types and symbols of religion can never be too well or naturally portrayed, and that, to be effective, they need never be grotesque; that the noblest painting and the most perfect grouping on the stage (we link the two together because they are so nearly allied) are modelled closely from nature, and keep to the simplest forms.

Thus ended the Passion Play for 1870, which has never been acted so well before, and can never by any possibility be produced so well again. Ten years later the extraordinary simplicity of character of these men will have worn off by contact with the outer world; they will have been praised too highly, and will know too much. In these days of photography, newspapers, railway communication, and "interviewing," it will be impossible for Joseph Mair, or his successor in the part, to study as calmly for the great character when it is reproduced in 1880. Every ten years there will be *more acting* and *less individuality* by force of circumstances and the weakness of human nature. Lang, who took the part of Caiaphas, is an instance of the kind of over-acting that is most to be feared, as the men become better educated and know more of the world. Two boys, members of the Lang family, have been educated at Munich and at Baden-Baden; and if it should come to their turn to take part in this play, their previous education will have been very different from that of Joseph Mair the wood-carver.

With the departure of Mair to the wars, we felt that the mysterious spell was broken, and that before ten years had passed away, we should have become—

> "too faithless or too wise
> For this old tale of many mysteries."

Let us take a last leaf from our note-book in 1870. It is now September; we are in Munich again, and the leaves are falling fast. For many weeks men's minds have been absorbed in nothing but war, and the streets of Munich are filled with troops day and night, going gaily to battle, as some one quaintly says, "with lighter hearts than they go to marriages."

This evening the whole city is abroad, and the war cloud that has hung over Munich so long shows its silver lining at last. Intelligence of victory after victory over the French has come in—with the long rolls of dead and dying—and at last a great hope of peace. Every public garden and place of meeting is crowded with people, and decorated for public rejoicing. We take our places as usual at one of the tables in the garden of the *Café National*, surrounded by people of all nations, including many American and English travellers. The noise is deafening, and the smoke hangs over us like a pall.

There are crowds of people passing to and fro outside the gates, and amongst the throng there is one face that we know well—it is Joseph Mair. He is dressed in the costume of modern civilisation—his "coat without seam" has been put away for a time, and his noble figure appears as ungainly as that of any man who dwells in cities! His long dark hair still falls in waves over his shoulders, but in modern attire his dignity and grace are gone! Let us hope that, when the war is over, he will return to Oberammergau as simple and pure in heart as when he left his native hills.[1]

It was the last sight of the 'Christus,' for he passed quickly away; and it was well for him to be gone, for the strains of Gungl's band, and the odour of *Lagerbier* with which the dusty trees of the garden were laden, tainted the breath of evening. The carousal was a national and a heavy one, and was carried well into the night. There they sat, men and women, in

---

[1] Mair worked out his term of service in 1870 at one of the military depôts at Munich; by special permission from the king he did not go into active service.

bright festal attire, whilst the full moon rose upon them. They were not uproarious, or badly behaved, and the majority went safely home; but some, it must be told, succumbed to patriotic influences, and bowed their heads like flowers full-blown.

We were "at home" again in Munich, there was no doubt of it. Did we not sometimes wish ourselves back in the Bavarian Tyrol? Did not some of us wish for the day when we might again study "Art in the Mountains."

Programme

OF THE

SCENES AND TABLEAUX OF THE PASSION PLAY.

PART I.

Tableaux.

1. Adam and Eve expelled from Paradise.
2. Angels bring glad tidings.
3. The sons of Jacob conspire against Joseph.
4. Tobias takes leave of his father.
5. The bride, surrounded by her handmaidens, laments the loss of the bridegroom.
6. King Ahasuerus, Esther, and Vashti.
7.
8. } The children of Israel receiving manna from Heaven.
9. Joseph sold to the Midianites.
10. Adam tilling the ground.
11. Joab embraces Amasa and kills him.

Scenes.

1. Christ enters Jerusalem, expels the money-changers from the Temple, and departs from Bethany.
2. The Court of the Sanhedrim take counsel together to put Christ to death.
3. The journey to Bethany and the supper at the house of Simon—Christ takes leave of his mother and his friends.
4. The journey to Jerusalem —Judas tempted to betray the Christ.
5. The Last Supper.
6. Judas sells his Master.
7. The Garden of Gethsemane—Judas betrays his Master—Christ is seized by the soldiers and led away.

PART II.

Tableaux.	Scenes.
12. Micaiah the prophet before Ahab and Jehoshaphat.	8. Christ brought before Annas.
13. Naboth stoned to death.	9. Christ before Caiaphas—Peter's denial of his Master, and repentance.
14. Job, seated by a well, taunted by his friends.	
15. The death of Abel.	10. The remorse and death of Judas.
16. Daniel before the court of Darius.	11. Christ before Pilate.
17. Samson in the Temple of Dagon.	12. Christ before Herod.
18. Joseph's brethren show the coat of many colours to Jacob.	13. Pilate orders Christ to be scourged—He is buffeted, and crowned with thorns.
19. Abraham about to sacrifice Isaac.	
20. Joseph richly clad, surrounded by the Egyptians.	14. Christ condemned to death.
21. The scapegoat.	
22. Abraham and Isaac go up to Mount Moriah.	15. The Way of the Cross—Women bewail their Lord.
23. ⎧ Moses shows the brazen serpent to the Israelites in the Wilderness. 24. ⎩	
(*No tableau.*)	16. The Crucifixion.
25. Jonah and the whale.	17. The Resurrection—Christ appears to Mary Magdalene.
26. Passage of the Red Sea.	
27. The Ascension into Heaven.	

Hallelujah Chorus.

LIST OF THE PRINCIPAL PERFORMERS IN 1870 AND IN 1880.

	1870.	1880.
THE CHRISTUS	*Joseph Mair.*	*Joseph Mair.*
PETER	*Jacob Hett.*	*Jacob Hett.*
JOHN	*Johannes Zwink.*	*Johannes Zwink.*
JUDAS	*Gregor Lechner.*	*Gregor Lechner.*
CAIAPHAS	*Johann Lang.*	*Johann Lang.*
PILATE	*Tobias Flunger.*	*Thomas Rendl.*
HEROD	*Franz Paul Lang.*	*Johann Rutz.*
ANNAS	*Gregor Stadler.*	*Sebastian Deschler.*
NATHANIEL	*Paul Fröschl.*	*Sebastian Lang.*
EZEKIEL	*Sebastian Deschler.*	*Rochus Lang.*
JOSEPH	*Thomas Rendl.*	*Martin Oppenrieder.*
NICODEMUS	*Anton Haafer.*	*Franz Steinbacher.*
BARABBAS	*Johann Allinger.*	*Johann Allinger.*
THE MARIA	*Franziska Flunger.*	*Anastasia Krach.*
MARY MAGDALENE	*Josepha Lang.*	*Maria Lang.*
LEADER OF THE CHORUS	*Johann Diemer.*	*Johann Diemer.*
CONDUCTOR OF THE ORCHESTRA	*Joseph Gutzjell.*	*Jos. Alois Kirschenhofer.*

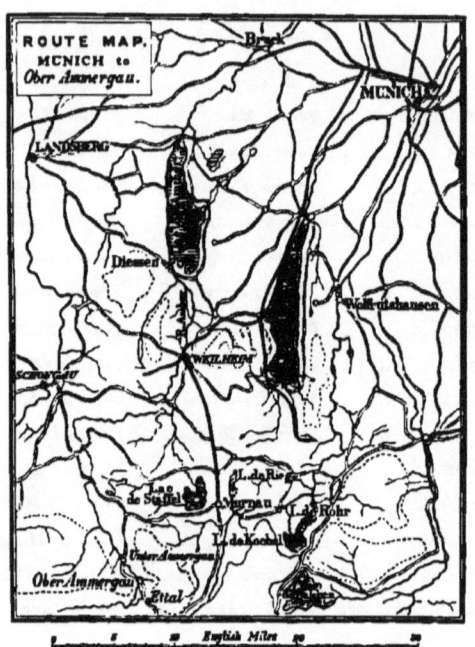

ROUTE FROM MUNICH TO OBERAMMERGAU.
By railway to MURNAU; thence by road, via ETTAL.

INFORMATION FOR TRAVELLERS.

THE quickest and easiest route from England is by Belgium and the Rhine to Munich. The cost of the double journey between London and Munich (return tickets lasting thirty days) varies from £7 to £12 by railway; but it is possible to travel more economically via Rotterdam and the Rhine steamers.

From Munich to Murnau is 63 miles, a journey of about three hours by railway; from Murnau to Oberammergau the distance is 24 kilometres (14 miles) partly over a steep mountain road. This latter part of the journey, from Murnau to Oberammergau, need not cost more than 3s. or 4s., as public conveyances meet the trains at Murnau.

There will be excursion trains on Saturdays from Munich (including the diligence to Oberammergau), at moderate fares; and it is proposed this year to run a late train from Murnau, to enable travellers to sleep at Munich on the night of the play.

The following are the dates of the Passion Play, as at present arranged.

MAY 17th, 23rd, 27th, and 30th.
JUNE 6th, 13th, 16th, 20th, 24th, and 27th.
JULY 4th, 11th, 18th, and 25th.
AUGUST 1st, 8th, 15th, 22nd, and 29th.
SEPTEMBER 5th, 8th, 12th, 19th, and 26th.

The performances commence at 8 A.M. and end at 5 P.M., with an hour's interval in the middle of the day.

The charges for admission to the theatre range from 1s. to 8s.; those at 5s., 6s., and 8s., being numbered and reserved, should be engaged before arriving at Oberammergau. The new theatre will accommodate nearly six thousand persons, the greater part being uncovered. There are 100 rows of seats, those at the back being raised and covered in. It is estimated that the new theatre and costumes have cost the commune more than £3000; and that the number of persons engaged in the performances, including children, is nearly 700.

The difficulties of obtaining accommodation at Oberammergau at the time of these performances have been rather exaggerated. Although Oberammergau is a mountain village, it contains a large number of houses fitted up with beds on purpose for visitors. The majority of these houses are well built, clean, and quiet, and there are uniform charges for beds and living throughout the village—5*s.* or 6*s.* a day. These charges, as well as the admission to the theatre, are not increased on the most crowded days.

It is advisable to *write beforehand* to Oberammergau to one of the principal persons in the village, stating what beds and places in the theatre are required; and also (to *insure* accommodation) to arrive there not later than the previous Friday. On one occasion, in June 1870, when the writer was present, about two thousand persons were turned from the theatre, the majority having to sleep in waggons, in sheds, or on the ground, and to wait for a second performance, which took place on the Monday.

There is a central bureau in the village for providing accommodation for travellers (in connection with the principal hotels in Munich), but some of the best people to write to, direct, are Madame Georg Lang; Sebastian Veit; George Igwinck; J. G. Rutz; or Tobias Flunger. At the houses of Georg Lang and Sebastian Veit, French is spoken, but all letters and communications should be made, if possible, in German.

It should be stated that there is now telegraphic communication with the village of Oberammergau, and that Messrs. Cook and Sons act as agents in London for securing accommodation.

The above remarks apply more especially to the four months in the summer of those years when the Passion Play is held at

Oberammergau; but as many people will probably visit the Bavarian highlands at other times, it may be useful to state that visitors can always stay in this pleasant mountain village, either at the inn, or at the house of Widow Lang.

Oberammergau is only a few miles from Partenkirch, Mittenwald, and the old post-road between Munich and Innsbruck. Travellers from the south can reach Oberammergau from Innsbruck in one day, by diligence. Posting is expensive and unnecessary, as there is a public conveyance daily to within five miles of the village. There are good inns at Murnau, Partenkirch, and Mittenwald.

Travellers in Switzerland (or coming from the west) may approach Oberammergau by the Lake of Constance to Lindau; and by railway to Kempten or Immenstadt. From Kempten it takes twelve or fourteen hours by the ordinary road; but it is better to take two days, sleeping at Reute. There is a beautiful carriage-road thence through the King's Forest (by the Plansee) to Oberammergau.

We should add, for the information of those who might prefer a novel and primitive method of travelling, that a large raft is floated down the river to Munich about once a week in the summer, by which travellers can return to Munich from Oberammergau for a few pence.

'The Homes of Oberammergau,' by Eliza Greatorex, published by J. Albert of Munich, contains an interesting account of the home life of the people, with sketches made in the district during a long visit.

H. B.

Books by the same Author.

'ARTISTS AND ARABS.'

'NORMANDY PICTURESQUE.'

'TRAVELLING IN SPAIN.'

'THE PYRENEES.'

'THE HARZ MOUNTAINS.'

'BRETON FOLK.'

Published by SAMPSON LOW & Co.
Crown Buildings, Fleet Street, London.

Just published, imperial 8vo., cloth extra, 21s.

Breton Folk

An Artistic Tour in Brittany.

WITH

ONE HUNDRED AND SEVENTY ILLUSTRATIONS BY
RANDOLPH CALDECOTT;

A NEW MAP OF ROUTES, AND INFORMATION FOR TRAVELLERS.

Opinions of the Press on 'Breton Folk.'

"*This handsome volume is the result of a three years' tour in Brittany by Mr. Henry Blackburn, who was accompanied for two seasons by Mr. Randolph Caldecott. The tourist who intends to visit Brittany might do much worse than take this joint production of Messrs. Blackburn and Caldecott with him; not only will he find pleasure in its literary and artistic merits, but he will learn from its pages a quantity of general information about the country. He will learn about hotels and their charges, routes and conveyances, the rivers that may be fished in, and the country that may be shot over. Mr. Caldecott's sketches are characterised by discrimination, humour, and clever drawing; he has caught the principal characteristics of the Breton, man, woman, and child, with great felicity.*"—Standard.

"*Messrs. Blackburn and Caldecott have been over the greatest part of Brittany, and they have made journey and sojourn nearly always with freshness of interest and freshness of mind and eye. The excellence of the book is the result of this. Mr. Blackburn's information in 'Breton Folk' is not hackneyed, and Mr. Caldecott's illustrations give us a very true revelation of Breton character and of Breton scenery.*"—Academy.

"'*Breton Folk' is the pleasant result of an artistic tour in Brittany* * * * *To say that the volume contains one hundred and seventy drawings by Mr. Caldecott is perhaps to say enough, for no contemporary artist combines so much truth with such unstrained and unaffected humour. Here, in short, is the whole life of the people displayed, ut in votiva tabella. Mr. Blackburn's part of the book is so good, and written in a style so pleasant and unforced, that the work is that very rare thing—a Christmas book which may be, and should be, read with serious attention.*"—Saturday Review.

"*Amongst all the merits of Mr. Henry Blackburn's volume, the chief, unless we are much mistaken, will be found to lie in the fact that it has been illustrated by Mr. Caldecott. And wonderful illustrations they are! As we turn them over we feel almost as though we must have unconsciously made a third in one of these summer tours in quiet, quaint old Brittany. To set aside the rare artistic merit of his work, in humour, in the faculty of selection, in ease without carelessness, in finish without laboriousness, it is long since so consummate a master has appeared in this particular field of art.*"—Times.

"*Mr. Caldecott's bright and animated vignettes are invariably welcome.*"—Athenæum.

OPINIONS OF THE PRESS (continued).

"The 'Artistic Tour in Brittany,' which bears the title of 'Breton Folk,' is a brilliant and sparkling work. The text has been written with good taste, and Mr. Caldecott has contributed a large number of spirited illustrations."—**Guardian.**

"Artist and author have told us what they saw and heard, and have given us a faithful record of some phases of actual life in a curiously old-world corner of France. The whole volume, both letterpress and pictures, will prove of great interest to travellers going to Brittany and to those who have already scraped some acquaintance with Breton folk."—**Spectator.**

"It is difficult to say which part is the more charming, the pleasant reading which accompanies Mr. Caldecott's sketches, or the delightful sketches which illustrate the text."—**Examiner.**

"Artist and author tracked the peasant in all parts of Brittany, exploring the out of the way nooks and corners unknown to tourists, and the harvest of their travels may be ranked as one of the brightest and most original volumes on Brittany."—**Graphic.**

"Author and artist could not be more happily matched than in this truly charming volume. The book is daintily got up, and thoroughly redolent of the fresh air. The illustrations are natural and humorous, and Mr. Blackburn shews at every turn that he has caught, as few travellers could catch, the genius of the life of a people from whom the charm of primitiveness has not yet departed."—**World.**

"Written with a fresh and joyous touch, charmingly suggestive of a careless holiday, and illustrated with rare delicacy and humour, this choicely printed volume deserves a foremost place amongst the art-books of the season."—**Truth.**

"Pen and pencil are worthily represented by Messrs. Blackburn and Caldecott in 'Breton Folk.' * * * The book is the perfection of simple and elegant taste, reflecting the highest credit on the judgment and enterprise of the publishers."—**Daily Telegraph.**

"The book is designed to take its place amongst the choicest of Christmas books."—**Art Journal.**

"When Mr. Blackburn's labours are joined to those of Mr. Caldecott, it is unnecessary to say how perfect is the result."—**Morning Post.**

"'Breton Folk' is a most pleasant and delightful volume of sketches of the people, of their habitations, costumes and customs."—**Queen.**

"The text of 'Breton Folk' is as interesting as any novel."—**Scotsman.**

"'Breton Folk' is a delightful book."—**Daily News.**

Etc. etc.

www.ingramcontent.com/pod-product-compliance
Lightning Source LLC
Chambersburg PA
CBHW022118160426
43197CB00009B/1077